OUR SOLAR SYSTEM

Saturn

BY DANA MEACHEN RAU

Content Adviser: Dr. Stanley P. Jones, Assistant Director, Washington, D.C., Operations, NASA Classroom of the Future

Science Adviser: Terrence E. Young Jr., M.Ed., M.L.S., Jefferson Parish (La.) Public Schools

Reading Adviser: Dr. Linda D. Labbo, Department of Reading Education, College of Education, The University of Georgia

COMPASS POINT BOOKS
MINNEAPOLIS, MINNESOTA

For Dad

Compass Point Books
3722 West 50th Street, #115
Minneapolis, MN 55410

Visit Compass Point Books on the Internet at *www.compasspointbooks.com*
or e-mail your request to *custserv@compasspointbooks.com*

Photographs ©: PhotoDisc, cover, 1, 3, 4–5, 10–11, 17 (all); Roger Ressmeyer/Corbis, 6; Scala/Art Resource, N.Y., 7; Hulton/Archive by Getty Images, 8 (top inset), 15; Corbis, 8 (bottom inset), 21, 22 (right); Astronomical Society of the Pacific, 8–9, 24–25; NASA/Roger Ressmeyer/Corbis, 12–13; Bettmann/Corbis, 14; NASA, 16, 18–19, 20, 22 (left); DigitalVision, 23.

Editors: E. Russell Primm and Emily J. Dolbear
Photo Researcher: Svetlana Zhurkina
Photo Selector: Dana Meachen Rau
Designer: The Design Lab
Illustrator: Graphicstock

Library of Congress Cataloging-in-Publication Data

Rau, Dana Meachen, 1971–
    Saturn / by Dana Meachen Rau.
        p. cm. — (Our solar system)
    Includes index.
    Summary: Briefly describes the surface features, composition, moons and rings,
and efforts to study the planet Saturn.
    ISBN 0-7565-0298-5 (hardcover)
    [1. Saturn (Planet)—Juvenile literature. 2. Saturn (Planet)] I. Title.
    QB384 .R38 2002
    523.46—dc21   2002002948

Table of Contents

Looking at
Saturn from Earth

Think of something that is very big. A car is big, and an elephant is big. Most things that are big are heavy, too. Saturn is very big! It could hold 764 Earths. But Saturn is very light for its size. If there were an ocean big enough to hold it, Saturn would float!

Saturn is the sixth planet from the Sun. People have known about Saturn for thousands of years. It is the second-largest planet. Only

◄ *Many people think Saturn is the most beautiful planet because of its unique rings.*

Jupiter is larger. Saturn can be seen easily from Earth without a **telescope**. It is one of the brightest objects in the sky. Some people think it is the most beautiful planet in the **solar system**.

Saturn looks pale yellow and shines bright like a star. People knew it wasn't a star because it didn't move in the sky the way stars do. The Romans called it *Saturn* after their god of planting.

Saturn is probably best known for its rings. Jupiter, Uranus, and Neptune also have rings. Saturn's rings are brightest. Italian **astronomer** Galileo Galilei (1564–1642) was one of the first people to see them. In 1610, he

When seen through a telescope, Saturn ▲ *appears to have a different shape from other planets because of its rings.*

Saturn was named after the ▶▶ *Roman god of planting.*

saw Saturn through his telescope. But he didn't know Saturn had rings. He thought Saturn was a "triple planet." It looked like Saturn had large lumps sitting on each side of it. In 1656, Dutch scientist Christiaan Huygens (1629–1695) used a stronger telescope to look at Saturn. He soon realized that Saturn was surrounded by rings.

The Italian astronomer ▶ Galileo (top) and the Dutch astronomer Christiaan Huygens (right) both studied Saturn in the 1600s.

Looking at the Way Saturn Moves

Saturn travels, or revolves, in a path around the Sun called an orbit. It takes Saturn about thirty Earth-years to make a trip around the Sun. Saturn also rotates while it revolves. To rotate means to spin. The planet is like a giant top. The northernmost point and the southernmost point of Saturn are called the poles.

Saturn rotates very fast. It takes Saturn only a little more than ten hours to spin around once. It takes Earth

◄ Saturn spins very quickly.

twenty-four hours to spin around once. And Earth is much smaller than Saturn. Ten hours is fast for such a large planet. Saturn's fast spin has flattened its poles. Unlike the other planets, Saturn does not look like a round ball. It looks slightly mushed.

Looking Through Saturn

⁑ Saturn is called a gas giant. That means it is made up mostly of gases. Jupiter, Uranus, and Neptune are also gas giant planets. These planets do not have hard surfaces like Earth. There is nowhere for people to stand—or for spacecraft to land—on a gas giant. Most of Saturn is made of hydrogen and helium.

Saturn probably has a hard rocky center, or **core**. This core is buried deep inside a layer of melted ice. Then

◀ *Saturn is made mostly of the gases hydrogen and helium.*

there is a thick cloudy atmosphere around the planet. A planet's atmosphere is made up of the gases around it.

The clouds in Saturn's atmosphere whip around the planet quickly. These clouds are blown by strong winds. Some winds blow at more

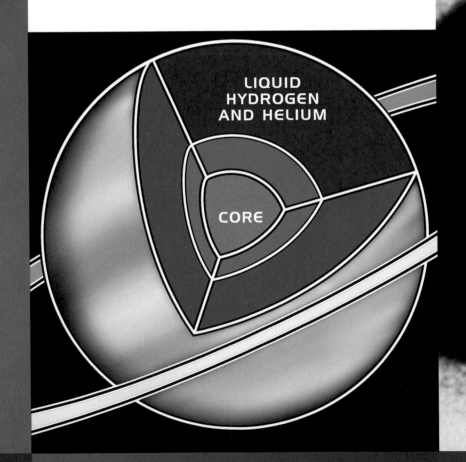

LIQUID
HYDROGEN
AND HELIUM

CORE

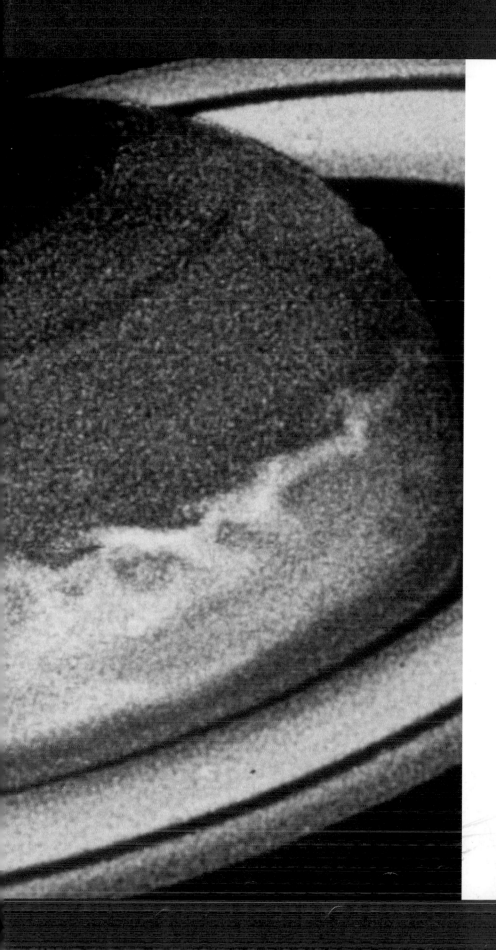

than 1,100 miles (1,770 kilometers) per hour. People
can sometimes see these
windstorms from Earth. They
look white. Storms on Saturn
sometimes cover areas as
large as our Earth.

The **temperature** of Saturn
is cold at the tops of clouds,
about –200 degrees Fahren
heit (–130 degrees Celsius).
It is hot deep in the planet's
core, however. The temperature of the core is about
21,000 degrees Fahrenheit
(11,650 degrees Celsius).

◄ *The white swirls in this picture are
storms on the planet.*

Looking Around Saturn

At first, people thought Saturn had one solid ring. Then in 1675, astronomer Jean Dominique Cassini (1625–1712) noticed a space in the ring. In 1857, scientist James Maxwell (1831–1879) found that the rings were made up of chunks of ice and rock. Each piece of ice and rock orbits the planet like a little moon. Some of the pieces are tiny. Some

Jean Dominique Cassini (right) and James Maxwell (far right) made important discoveries about Saturn's rings.

are as big as a building.

Early scientists thought Saturn had only three rings. In 1974, however, scientists sent the *Pioneer 11* spacecraft to look at Saturn more closely. The spacecraft sent back close-up pictures of the rings. Then the scientists saw that there were hundreds of "ring-lets" around Saturn. These ringlets are grouped into about seven larger ring groups. The rings stretch about 170,000 miles (274,000 kilometers) around the planet. But they are only 1 mile (1.6 kilometers) thick.

▲ *This is a close-up view of the hundreds of ringlets circling Saturn.*

Scientists are interested in finding out how these rings formed. They might have once been moons. An object flying in space, such as an **asteroid** or a **comet**, might have hit the moons and broke them apart. Or the rings might be pieces of a comet that broke up when it flew too close to Saturn.

Moons also orbit around Saturn. Saturn has six large moons and many smaller ones. Twelve new moons were discovered in 2000. In all, Saturn has at least thirty unique and interesting

◄ *Some of Saturn's moons: Hyperion (top) is irregular in shape. Enceladus (middle) is bright. Dione (bottom) is covered with bright white streaks.*

moons. Enceladus is bright. Tethys looks like a giant ball of ice. Dione has bright wispy marks crossing its surface. Iapetus is dark in some parts and light in others. Hyperion wobbles as it orbits. Mimas has a huge crater on its surface that covers almost half of the planet.

Titan is the most interesting moon. It is Saturn's largest moon. It is also the second-largest moon in the solar system. (Jupiter's Ganymede is larger.) It is the only moon in the solar system with a large atmosphere.

Each of Saturn's many moons is ▸ unique and interesting.

Looking at Saturn from Space

✦ *Pioneer 11* was the first spacecraft to visit Saturn. It was launched in 1974. It arrived at Saturn in 1979 after flying by Jupiter. *Pioneer 11* sent back the first pictures of Saturn's astounding rings. It took many other pictures of Saturn, too. When *Pioneer 11* was done, it head-ed off into space.

In 1980 and 1981, *Voyager 1* and *Voyager 2* also flew by Saturn. The *Voyager* space-craft were sent to study all

Workers prepare Pioneer 11 *for its ▶ trip into space.*

the gas giant planets. Every 189 years, Jupiter, Saturn, Uranus, and Neptune are close to one another. They are lined up in a way that makes it easier for spacecraft to travel from one planet to the next. Scientists called the Voyager mission the "Grand Tour" of the gas giant planets. *Voyager 1* and *2* found more moons around Saturn. They also told scientists a lot more about that planet's mysterious rings.

Another spacecraft is now on its way to Saturn. *Cassini-*

▲ *Voyager 2 took pictures of Saturn's rings for scientists to study on Earth.*

Huygens was launched in 1997. It will arrive at Saturn in 2004. When *Cassini* arrives, it will drop a smaller spacecraft, named *Huygens*, toward Titan. Then *Cassini* will continue to orbit the planet for about four years. *Cassini* will gather information and take pictures of Saturn and its rings and moons.

Huygens is going to fall through the atmosphere of Titan. This will take about

▲ *On October 15, 1997,* Cassini *(above left) was launched into space for its seven-year trip to Saturn.*

▲ Cassini *(above right) will study Saturn and its moons.*

two and a half hours. As it falls, *Huygens* will gather facts about the atmosphere and take pictures. Three parachutes will help the **probe** float down to the surface. Scientists don't know what that surface will be like. *Huygens* may fall onto rock or ice. It may splash into liquid. It may crash or sink when it lands. If it is still in good shape, it will continue to gather facts for another two hours or so.

◀ *The probe* Huygens *will drop through Titan's atmosphere to the surface.*

Looking to the Future

★ Scientists have many questions about Saturn. They want to know how the rings were formed. They want to know why Saturn's rings are so different from those of the other gas giants. They hope that *Cassini-Huygens* will answer many of their questions.

Scientists are especially eager to find out about Titan. Some people believe Titan may look like Earth did

*Future study of Saturn, its rings, and ▶
its moons will answer many questions
about Saturn, as well as questions
about our own planet.*

when it was being formed. The facts *Huygens* collects may tell us a lot about what Earth looked like billions of years ago.

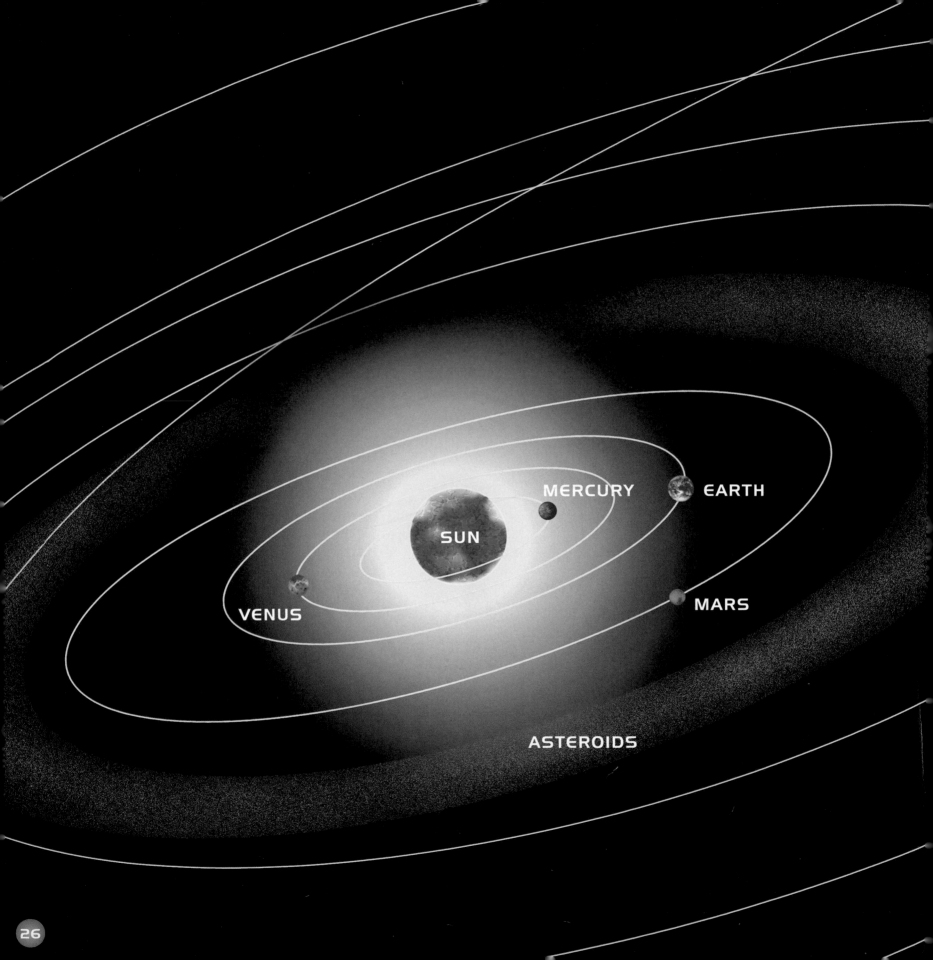

VENUS

MERCURY

EARTH

SUN

MARS

ASTEROIDS

JUPITER

URANUS

SATURN

NEPTUNE

PLUTO

Glossary

asteriod—a chunk of rock that orbits the Sun especially between the orbits of Mars and Jupiter

astronomer—someone who studies space

comet—a piece of ice and rock with a long tail of dust that orbits the Sun

core—the center of a planet

probe—part of a spacecraft that drops to the surface of a planet or moon

solar system—a group of objects in space including the Sun, planets, moons, asteroids, comets, and meteoroids

telescope—a tool astronomers use to make objects look closer

temperature—how hot or cold something is

A Saturn Flyby

Saturn is the second-largest planet and the sixth planet from the Sun.

If you weighed 75 pounds (34 kilograms) on Earth, you would weigh 75.5 pounds (34.3 kilograms) on Saturn.

Average distance from the Sun: 890 million miles (1,400 million kilometers)

Distance from Earth: 743 million miles: (1,196 million kilometers) to 1,031 million miles (1,659 million kilometers)

Diameter: 74,897 miles (120,509 kilometers)

Number of times Earth would fit inside Saturn: 764

Did You Know?

- Some important missions to Saturn include *Pioneer 11*, *Voyager 1*, *Voyager 2*, and *Cassini-Huygens*.

- *Pioneer 11* carries a plaque with a picture of Earth and people on it. In case there are other lifeforms in the universe, they would find the plaque and know where *Pioneer 11* was sent from and who sent it.

- The day we call *Saturday* is also named after the Roman god Saturn.

- Dark spokes on Saturn's rings form and then disappear. Scientists don't know why.

- Saturn's smallest moon, Pan, is 12 miles (19.3 kilometers) wide. Its largest moon, Titan, is 3,200 miles (5,150 kilometers) wide.

- Saturn's moon Titan is even larger than the planets Pluto and Mercury, and it is almost as big as Mars.

- Some of Saturn's rings have small moons that orbit on either side. These moons help keep the objects that make up rings in place.

Time it takes to orbit around Sun (one Saturn year): 29.5 Earth-years	Structure: core (rock or metal) liquid hydrogen	Atmosphere: hydrogen, helium	Moons: at least 30
			Rings: 7 ring groups
Time it takes to rotate (one Saturn day): 10.2 Earth-hours	Average temperature of cloud tops: –200° Fahrenheit (–130° Celsius)	Atmospheric pressure (Earth=1.0): unknown	

Want to Know More?

AT THE LIBRARY

Landau, Elaine. *Saturn*. Danbury, Conn.: Franklin Watts, 2000.

Mitton, Jacqueline, and Simon Mitton. *Scholastic Encyclopedia of Space*. New York: Scholastic Reference, 1998.

Redfern, Martin. *The Kingfisher Young People's Book of Space*. New York: Kingfisher, 1998.

Ridpath, Ian. *Stars and Planets*. New York: DK Publishing, Inc., 1998.

Vogt, Gregory. *Jupiter, Saturn, Uranus, and Neptune*. Austin, Tex.: Raintree/Steck-Vaughn, 2000.

ON THE WEB

Cassini-Huygens Mission to Saturn and Titan
http://saturn.jpl.nasa.gov/cassini/index.shtml
For up-to-date information about this mission

Exploring the Planets: Saturn
http://www.nasm.edu/ceps/etp/saturn/
For more information about Saturn

The Nine Planets: Saturn
http://www.seds.org/nineplanets/nineplanets/saturn.html
For a multimedia tour of Saturn

Solar System Exploration: Missions to Saturn
http://sse.jpl.nasa.gov/missions/sat_missns/sat-cassini.html
For more information about important NASA missions to Saturn

Space Kids
http://spacekids.hq.nasa.gov/
NASA's space-science site designed just for kids

Space.com
http://www.space.com
For the latest news about everything to do with space

Star Date Online: Saturn
http://www.stardate.org/resources/ssguide/saturn.html
For an overview of Saturn and hints on where it can be seen in the sky

Welcome to the Planets: Saturn
http://pds.jpl.nasa.gov/planets/choices/saturn1.htm
For pictures and information about Saturn and some of its most important surface features

THROUGH THE MAIL

Goddard Space Flight Center
Code 130, Public Affairs Office
Greenbelt, MD 20771
To learn more about space exploration

Jet Propulsion Laboratory
4800 Oak Grove Drive
Pasadena, CA 91109
To learn more about spacecraft missions

Lunar and Planetary Institute
3600 Bay Area Boulevard
Houston, TX 77058
To learn more about Saturn and
other planets

Space Science Division
NASA Ames Research Center
Moffet Field, CA 94035
To learn more about Saturn and
solar system exploration

ON THE ROAD

**Adler Planetarium and
Astronomy Museum**
1300 S. Lake Shore Drive
Chicago, IL 60605-2403
312/922-STAR
To visit the oldest planetarium
in the Western Hemisphere

***Exploring the Planets* and
*Where Next, Columbus?***
National Air and Space Museum
7th and Independence Avenue, S.W.
Washington, DC 20560
202/357-2700
To learn more about the solar system
at this museum exhibit

**Rose Center for Earth and
Space/Hayden Planetarium**
Central Park West at 79th Street
New York, NY 10024-5192
212/769-5100
To visit this new planetarium and
learn more about the planets

UCO/Lick Observatory
University of California
Santa Cruz, CA 95064
408/274-5061
To see the telescope that was used to
discover the first planets outside of
our solar system

Index

◄ **About the Author:** *Dana Meachen Rau loves to study space. Her office walls are covered with pictures of planets, astronauts, and spacecraft. She also likes to look up at the sky with her telescope and write poems about what she sees. Ms. Rau is the author of more than seventy-five books for children, including nonfiction, biographies, storybooks, and early readers. She lives in Burlington, Connecticut, with her husband, Chris, and children, Charlie and Allison.*